Man-To-Man Talk

AF624535

ILYA BLOYE

BookLeaf Publishing

Presentation by *BookLeaf Publishing*

Web: www.bookleafpub.com

E-mail: info@bookleafpub.com

ISBN: 9789357214117

First edition 2023

My First December Poem

Twas a misty time, on a Monday morning
A man stood, for he was mourning
A loss on Christmas Eve, a friend...
God, make this dam war end!

My Second December Poem

A new generation,
They look at the screen.
They ignore all they hear,
And don't want to be seen.

My Third December Poem

The money in his pocket,
It jingles, jangles, jingles.
The lad down the road
Just bought a pack'o pringles.

My Fourth December Poem

World leaders sit at a table,
A map of the world lays in front of them.
They play their twisted game of soldiers,
Who cares who lives and who dies?...

My Fifth December Poem

The world keeps on spinning,
And a lot of us are fine.
But even if it's not,
It's a great thing, Life!

My Sixth December Poem

The wind whistled loudly,
And the rain pored heavily.
A man stood there and said:
"Ah, a good English day! Lovely"

My Seventh December Poem

A piano trainee plays the instrument,
Plank, plink, plank.
The trainer sighs and shakes his head,
Plank, plink, plank.

My Eighth December Poem

Europeans speak gobble de goop,
And its the same for the globe.
So no wonder it's a common question:
Why do different languages exist?

My Ninth December Poem

Pasta and pizza,
They're such yummy pleasures.
But, as all things in life,
They are greater in measures.

My Tenth December Poem

The teen sits at a PC,
The adult at a TV.
No-one ever seems to have time,
Nor for pets, nor for tea.

My Eleventh December Poem

A man sat in a rocking chair,
He rocked to and fro,
Oh, he had seen so many things,
From being called "Sir",
to being called "Bro".

My Twelfth December Poem

I love water, and I'll tell you why,
I'll explain it so much it might make you cry,
But the taste is so simple, so empty, so plain,
That I love it enough even to drink it on a plane.

My Thirteenth December Poem

It's snowing, it's snowing, it's snowing,
Its snowing enough for a pie.
It's snowing, it's snowing, it's snowing,
Alright, that's enough, goodbye.

My Fourteenth December Poem

A boy sat in bed, phone in hand,
Playing games that brought him pleasure,
And thought to himself, whilst sipping warm tea,
"Ah, a great thing, leisure."

My Fifteenth December Poem

The man looked out the window,
And felt a great joy,
And memories came back,
Of parties and toys,
So it just goes to show, big or small,
Christmas is a time loved by all!

My Sixteenth December Poem

The music roared through the hall,
And people played Hip Hop and other malarky,
And in this giant mess of celebration,
People really know how to party!

My Seventeenth December Poem

Dogs, they come in varying shapes and sizes,
In many breeds, colours and different colour
eyes,
But what a pet dog truly needs,
Is a heart and soul the size of a pine tree.

My Eighteenth December Poem

The ice thawed and cracked away,
The snow evaporates and melts.
A farmer might cheer, a student might gloom,
But that's England for you, me mates.

My Nineteenth December Poem

Are there miracles?... Good question,
For any Aristotles out there,
The answer could be bitter,
Or as delicious as a pear.
For miracles can happen just like that,
Or only when you're out in Costa,
But, as the Russians may put it,
"А это, друг, не так-то просто."

My Twentieth December Poem

A Christmas Carol is one of the best,
Ask Dave, ask Bob, ask Pickens.
And people might even after many centuries, say
"Good Job, Dickens!"

My Twenty-First December Poem

Christmas! A time of cheer,
Of gifting, of loving, of supporting all,
So maybe, just maybe, I can get away with
rhyming this with "all":
Merry Christmas, one and all!

www.ingramcontent.com/pod-product-compliance
Lightning Source LLC
Chambersburg PA
CBHW062112140826
49812CB00058B/1311
* 9 7 8 9 3 5 7 2 1 4 1 1 7 *